Making History
A Covered Wagon

Victoria Braidich

The Tony Stead
NONFICTION
INDEPENDENT
READING COLLECTION

Rosen Classroom Books & Materials™
New York

Published in 2006 by The Rosen Publishing Group, Inc.
29 East 21st Street, New York, NY 10010

Copyright © 2006 by The Rosen Publishing Group, Inc.

All rights reserved. No part of this book may be reproduced in any form without permission in writing from the publisher, except by a reviewer.

First Edition

Book Design: Michael Tsanis

Photo Credits: Front/back cover, pp. 14, 17, 18, 20, 21, 22 by Pablo Maldonado; p. 5 © North Wind Picture Archives; p. 6 © Charlie Borland/Index Stock; pp. 7, 9 © Bettman/Corbis; p. 13 © Corbis.

Library of Congress Cataloging-in-Publication Data

Braidich, Victoria.
  Making history : a covered wagon / Victoria Braidich.
    p. cm. — (The Tony Stead nonfiction independent reading collection)
  Includes index.
  ISBN 1-4042-5589-3 (pbk.)
  Theme ISBN: 1-4042-6314-4
 1. Overland journeys to the Pacific—Juvenile literature. 2. Overland journeys to the Pacific—Study and teaching (Primary—Activity programs. 3. Wagon trains—West (U.S.)—History—19th century—Juvenile literature. 4. Wagon trains—West (U.S.) —History—19th century—Study and teaching (Primary—Activity programs. 5. West (U.S.)—Description and travel—Juvenile literature. 6. West (U.S.)—Description and travel—Study and teaching (Primary)—Activity programs. I. Title. II. Series.
  F593.B745 2005
  917.8—dc22

2005007848

Manufactured in the United States of America

Contents

The Move West 4
Covered Wagons 7
Flatboats 8
On the Trail 11
The End of the Trail 12
Covered Wagon Model 15
Starting Your Covered Wagon 16
Finishing Your Covered Wagon 20
Remembering Life on the Trail 22
Glossary 23
Index 24
Web Sites 24

The Move West

Between 1760 and 1860, American **pioneers** made new paths across the country. Many of the pioneers traveled west in covered wagons. At first, people went as far as the Mississippi River. They settled on the land alongside the river. When that area became too crowded, pioneers went farther and farther west in search of open land.

Pioneer families had to carry food, supplies, and belongings in their covered wagons. The wagons were almost like houses on wheels.

5

Covered Wagons

canvas cover

Most of the covered wagons the pioneers traveled in were about 10 to 12 feet (3 to 3.7 m) long. These wagons could carry up to 2,500 pounds (1,134 kg). The wagon's cover was made out of **canvas**. Sometimes women and children rode inside the wagon. Sometimes they walked because the wagon was too crowded, or because it was already too heavy for the animals to pull.

It took about 4 to 6 months for pioneers to reach the west coast when traveling by covered wagon.

Flatboats

Some pioneers traveled west by floating on the Ohio River in a flatboat. A flatboat is a large, flat raft with a cabin built on top. The pioneers needed the cabin to **protect** themselves and their belongings from unpleasant weather. It was a good way to travel if you could get where you wanted to go by river. More pioneers traveled by covered wagon than by flatboat because covered wagons could reach more places.

Pioneers who needed to travel on rivers to get where they wanted to go used flatboats.

On the Trail

Most pioneers traveled west on trails. The **Oregon Trail** and the **Santa Fe Trail** were two main trails leading west. Both trails started in Independence, Missouri. While traveling, many pioneers, both children and adults, kept journals. These trail journals are now important historical **documents** that tell us how hard life could be on the journey west.

This map shows the Oregon and Santa Fe trails.

The End of the Trail

The Oregon Trail reached a town in Oregon called The Dalles. From here, many pioneers loaded their covered wagons onto boats and made a dangerous journey down the Columbia and Willamette Rivers to Oregon City. Starting in 1845, many pioneers took the equally dangerous Barlow Trail through the Cascade Mountains. Some pioneers settled in and around Oregon City. Others traveled on to places along the northern Pacific coast.

This picture, taken in the early 1900s, shows descendants of Oregon Trail pioneers posing near a monument in The Dalles, Oregon, marking the end of the Oregon Trail.

Covered Wagon Model

You can make your own covered wagon model. You will need the following tools and materials:
- ★ piece of cardboard, $8\frac{1}{2}$ inches by 11 inches (21.6 cm by 27.9 cm)
- ★ scissors
- ★ sheet of white paper
- ★ top of cardboard box (shoebox or smaller)
- ★ tape
- ★ four brass tacks
- ★ paint
- ★ paintbrush
- ★ two pieces of yarn, 8 inches (20 cm) each
- ★ two small plastic horses

Starting Your Covered Wagon

Step 1:

Cut four circles out of the cardboard. Each circle should be $3\frac{1}{2}$ inches (8.9 cm) across. Cut a piece of white paper lengthwise so that the short sides fit inside the box top when it is put in place as shown. Poke a hole with the scissors near each end of the box top's long sides. Now poke a hole in the center of each cardboard wheel. Remember to be careful when using scissors.

17

18

Step 2:

Tape the white paper to the box top so that it forms a curved shape covering the box top. Put a brass tack in the center hole of each wheel, and then push it into one of the holes on the sides of the box top. This will hold your wagon's wheels in place.

Finishing Your Covered Wagon

Step 3:

Paint the wagon and wagon wheels and let them dry. Leave the curved paper white so it looks like a canvas top on the wagon.

Step 4:

Use the yarn to tie the horses to the wagon. (Often travelers used oxen instead of horses.) Now you're ready for the trail!

Remembering Life on the Trail

The covered wagon played a very important role in the history of the United States. The covered wagon you just made can be displayed as a reminder of this period of growth and adventure.

Glossary

canvas (KAN-vuhs) A strong, heavy cloth, often made of cotton.

document (DAH-kyuh-muhnt) A written or printed record, such as a journal or diary.

Oregon Trail (OR-ih-guhn TRAYL) A trail connecting Independence, Missouri, and Oregon City, Oregon. Many pioneers used it to travel west.

pioneer (py-uh-NEER) One of the first people to settle in a new area.

protect (pruh-TEKT) To keep something or someone safe from harm.

Santa Fe Trail (SAN-tuh FAY TRAYL) A trail connecting Independence, Missouri, and Santa Fe, New Mexico. Many pioneers used it to travel west.

Index

B
Barlow Trail, 12

C
Cascade Mountains, 12
Columbia River, 12

D
Dalles, The, 12

F
flatboat, 8

I
Independence, Missouri, 11

J
journals, 11

M
Mississippi River, 4

O
Ohio River, 8
Oregon, 12
Oregon City, 12
Oregon Trail, 11, 12

P
Pacific coast, 12
pioneers, 4, 7, 8, 11, 12

S
Santa Fe Trail, 11

U
United States, 22

W
Willamette River, 12

Web Sites

Due to the changing nature of Internet links, the Rosen Publishing Group, Inc., has developed an online list of Web sites related to the subject of this book. This site is updated regularly. Please use this link to access the list:

http://www.rcbmlinks.com/tsirc/covwagon/